Want to know
nature

My Body

Pierre Winters & Eline van Lindenhuizen

Clavis

NEW YORK

Laura and Sam are playing outside.
They're wearing lots of clothes:
Boots, coats, a sweater, a scarf.
Do you know what's underneath all those clothes?

Your body! Your body exists of lots of different parts.
Do you know the names of all your body parts?

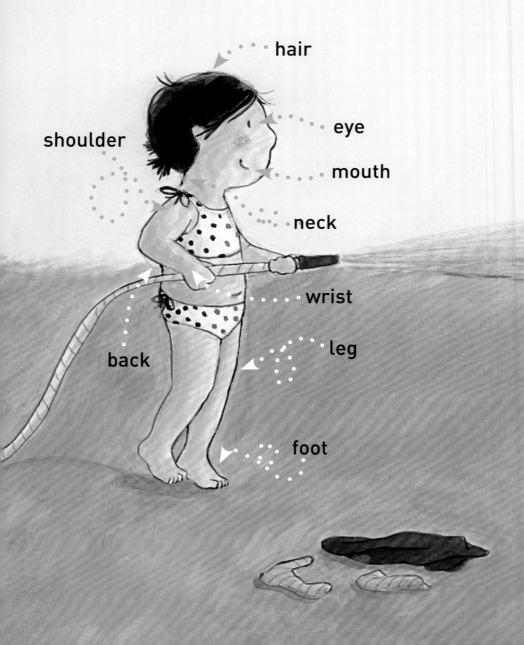

hair

eye

shoulder

mouth

neck

wrist

back

leg

foot

head

nose

ear

stomach

arm

elbow

finger

hand

knee

ankle

toe

Your face

The features of your face show who you are and what you feel.
There are many kinds of faces—short and long faces,
round and narrow faces. Your face also shows others how you feel

Did you know
that no face
is the same as your face?
Every face is different.

What expressions do you see on these faces?

happy

sad

scared

surprised

impertinent

shy

sleepy

angry

grumpy

Eyes

You can see with your two eyes.
Eyes allow you to see the world, read books, and watch television.
Your eyes also make tears sometimes.

What color are your eyes: brown, blue, green, or gray?
If you can't see that well, you can get a pair of eyeglasses to help you.
When you're sad or in pain, your eyes create tears.
This is perfectly normal.

Did you know that in summer it is a good idea to wear sunglasses to protect your sensitive eyes from the bright rays of the sun?

Nose

Your nose helps you to breathe. It also allows you to smell things. Some things have a sweet and delicious smell, other things have a sharp and unpleasant smell.

Did you know that there are lots of tiny hairs inside your nose? These hairs stop dust from getting inside your body. Sometimes you sneeze when dust gets in your nose.

How do these things smell?

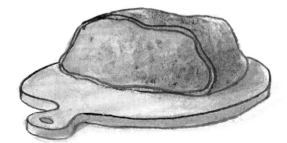

Mouth

You use your mouth to eat and to drink—and to talk.
Your mouth contains teeth, which bite and chew,
and a tongue to help you taste things.

What can you do with your mouth?

sing

shout

make silly faces

stick out your tongue

whistle

blow bubbles

kiss

gasp

laugh

Ears

You can hear with your two ears. What do you hear?
Some sounds are soft and some sounds are loud.

How do these things sound?

Muscles

Around your bones are strong muscles which help you move.
Muscles allow you to stretch and bend.

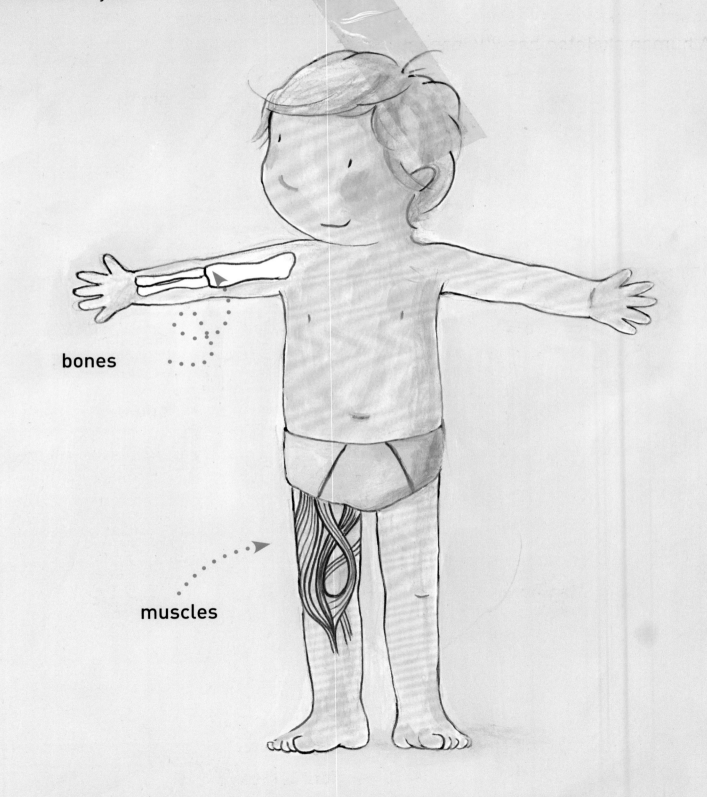

bones

muscles

Bones

Inside every single person there's a "skeleton" made up of hard bones. These bones give your body structure, let you move in many ways, and protect your internal organs. You can feel a lot of your bones under your skin. A human skeleton has 206 bones!

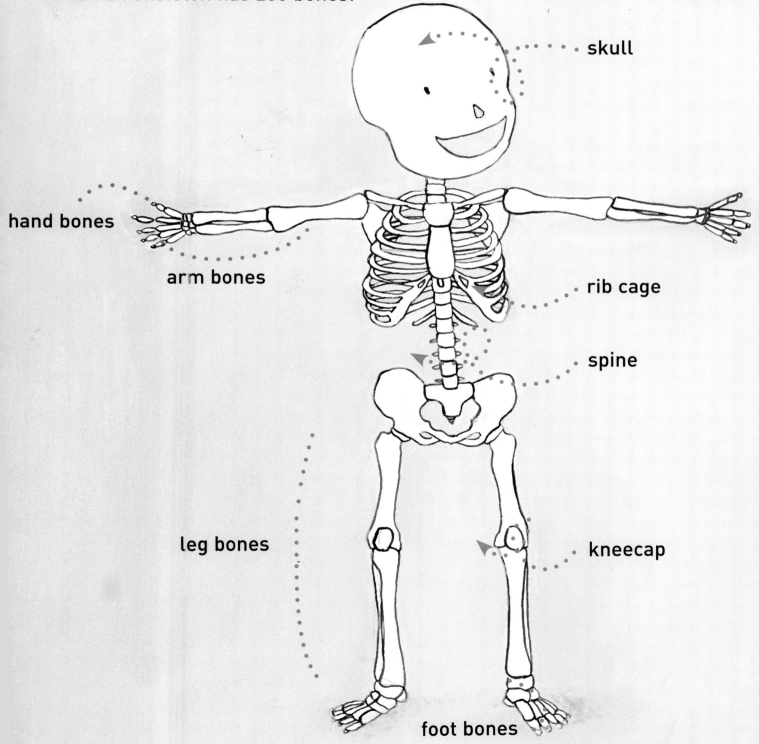

skull

hand bones

arm bones

rib cage

spine

leg bones

kneecap

foot bones

build

clap

stretch

Arms and hands

Your arms are attached to your shoulders.
Your hands are attached to your arms.
You can do many things with your hands and arms.
Look what Sam can do.

push

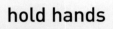

hold hands

stroke

Hair

Everyone's body is covered with hair. Most of the hair on your body grows on your head. Hair comes in many different colors. Some people have lots of hair and other people have a little hair. Having no hair is called being "bald." There are all sorts of hair styles: short, long, curly, straight, wavy, spiky. What kind of hair do you have?

Organs

There are very important "organs" in your body. They all work together, like parts of a machine, to keep you healthy. It's important to take good care of your organs. (Guess what? Your skin is an organ, too!)

Your **stomach** and intestines help move food and liquids through your body.

Your **lungs** allow you to breathe and get enough air into your body and blood.

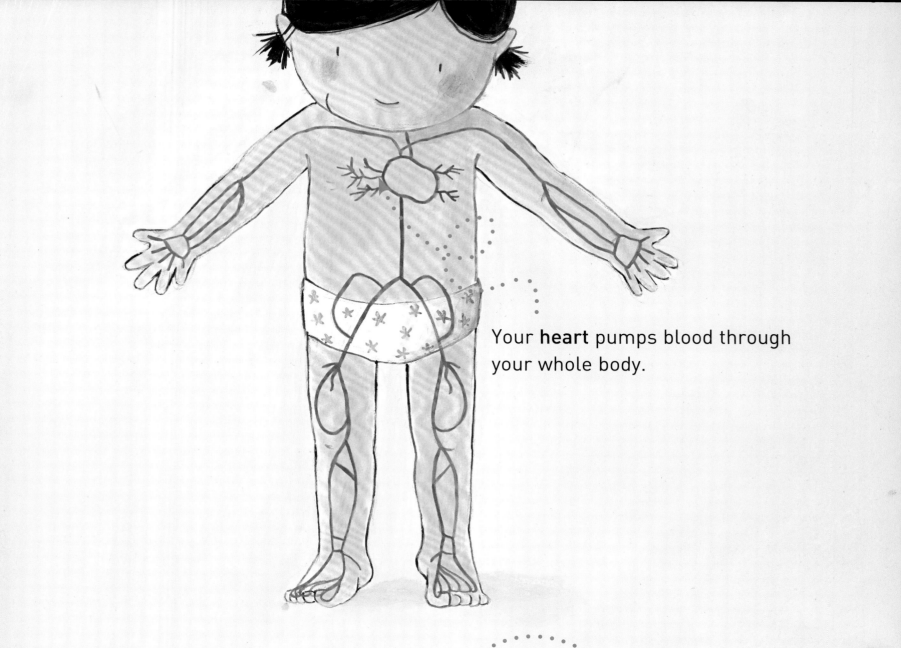

Your **heart** pumps blood through your whole body.

Your **brain** is like the boss of your body. It allows you to think and it sends messages to all your body parts so they know what to do.

run

dance

jump

Legs and feet

Your two legs and feet hold you up and allow you to move around. You can do many things with your legs and feet! Just look at Laura.

kick

stand on one leg

splash

Taking care of your body

Your body is the most important thing that you have and you only get one. So it's important to take very good care of it. Eat and drink healthy foods and liquids, but not too much.
Sleep deeply when you're tired and move around a lot when you're awake. If you feel cold, make sure to get warm. And if you feel warm, it's good to cool down. Keep yourself clean by taking a shower or bath regularly, brushing your teeth twice a day, brushing your hair, cutting your fingernails, and don't forget to clean behind your ears!

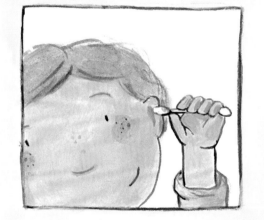
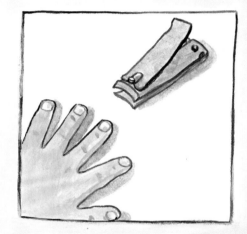

Clap! Clap! Stomp! Stomp!

Clap your hands—
Clap! Clap! Clap!
Stomp your feet—
Stomp! Stomp! Stomp!